KU-244-317

Watching Tree Frogs
in South America

Elizabeth Miles

Heinemann
LIBRARY

www.heinemann.co.uk/library

Visit our website to find out more information about Heinemann Library books.

To order:

 Phone 44 (0) 1865 888066

 Send a fax to 44 (0) 1865 314091

 Visit the Heinemann Bookshop at www.heinemann.co.uk/library to browse our catalogue and order online.

First published in Great Britain by Heinemann Library, Halley Court, Jordan Hill, Oxford OX2 8EJ, part of Harcourt Education. Heinemann is a registered trademark of Harcourt Education Ltd.

© Harcourt Education Ltd 2006
The moral right of the proprietor has been asserted.

All rights reserved. No part of this publication may be reproduced, stored in a retrieval system, or transmitted in any form or by any means, electronic, mechanical, photocopying, recording, or otherwise, without either the prior written permission of the Publishers or a licence permitting restricted copying in the United Kingdom issued by the Copyright Licensing Agency Ltd, 90 Tottenham Court Road, London WIT 4LP (www.cla.co.uk).

Editorial: Nancy Dickmann and Sarah Chappelow
Design: Ron Kamen and edesign
Illustrations: Martin Sanders
Picture Research: Maria Joannou and Christine Martin
Production: Camilla Crask
Originated by Modern Age
Printed and bound in Italy by Printer Trento srl

ISBN 0 431 19070 4
10 09 08 07 06
10 9 8 7 6 5 4 3 2 1

British Library Cataloguing in Publication Data
Miles, Elizabeth
Watching tree frogs in South America. – (Wild world)
597.8'7817'098
A full catalogue record for this book is available from the British Library.

Acknowledgements

The Publishers would like to thank the following for permission to reproduce the following photographs: Alamy p. 13 (ImageState); Corbis pp. 15 (David Aubrey), 25 (David A Northcott), 26 (Paulo Fridman), 28 (Dave G Houser), 29 (Keren Su); Digital Vision p. 5; FLPA pp. 4 (Mark Moffett), 5 (Michael & Patricia Fogden), 8 (Heidi & Hans-Juergen Koch), 16 (Michael & Patricia Fogden), 19 (Heidi & Hans-Juergen Koch), 20 (Heidi & Hans-Juergen Koch), 28; Getty Images pp. 7, 11, 14, 17; Nature PL pp. 12 (Martin Gabriel), 21 (Fabio Liverani), 24 (Barry Mansell); NHPA pp. 9 (Paulo de Oliveira), 22 (Daniel Heuclin), 27 (Mirko Stelzner); Photolibrary p. 18; PhotoLibrary.com p. 10 (Paulo de Oliveira); Science Photo Library p. 23. Cover photograph of a red-eyed tree frog reproduced with permission of Getty Images/Taxi/Gail Shumway.

The publishers would like to thank Michael Bright of the BBC Natural History Unit for his assistance in the preparation of this book.

Every effort has been made to contact copyright holders of any material reproduced in this book. Any omissions will be rectified in subsequent printings if notice is given to the publishers. The paper used to print this book comes from sustainable resources.

DUDLEY PUBLIC LIBRARIES

L

674193   SCH

J 597.8

Contents

Words written in bold, **like this**, are explained in the glossary.

Meet the tree frogs

This is South America, the home of red-eyed tree frogs. Tree frogs are small frogs. Like all frogs, they are **amphibians**. They can live in water or on land.

⏫ *Tree frogs live in places with lots of rain, and lots of places to hide.*

4

🔺 *This is a blue poison arrow frog.*

There are many different kinds of tree frog. They all look different. Some are brightly coloured. We are going to watch the red-eyed tree frogs.

South American rainforests

Red-eyed tree frogs are found in South America, Central America, and Mexico. They live in **rainforests**. A rainforest is a jungle where lots of rain falls.

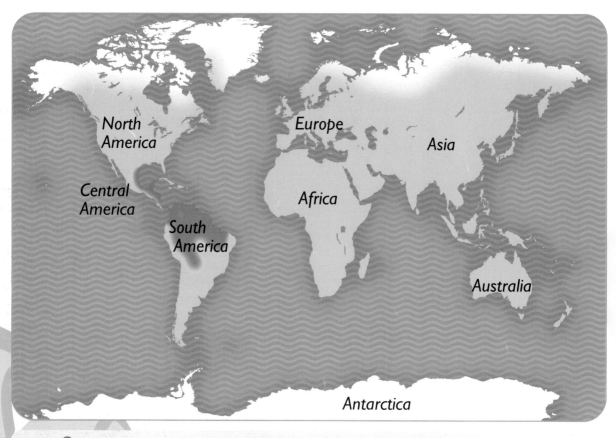

North America

Europe

Asia

Central America

Africa

South America

Australia

Antarctica

Key ● This colour shows where red-eyed tree frogs live in Central and South America.

Many trees and plants grow in a rainforest. A lot of rain falls. The water collects in pools, leaves, and flowers. This makes a perfect **habitat** for tree frogs.

▼ *Tree frogs need to live near pools of water. They lay their eggs there.*

There's a tree frog!

Red-eyed tree frogs are hard to spot.
They are smaller than a tennis ball.
They have red eyes, a green back,
and blue stripes.

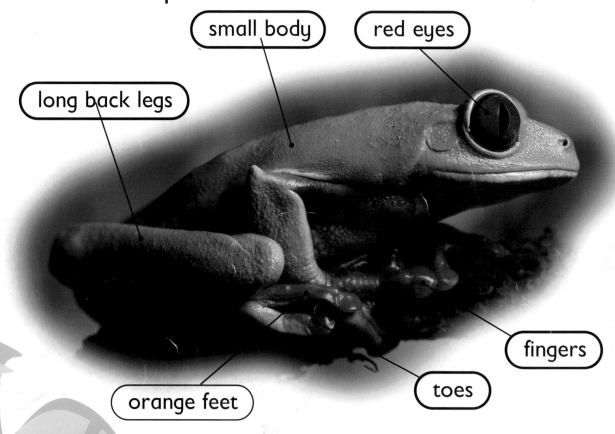

small body

red eyes

long back legs

fingers

toes

orange feet

▲ Like most frogs, the red-eyed
tree frog has smooth, wet skin.

Red-eyed tree frogs have toes and fingers that grip well. Their long back legs help them jump. Inside their wide mouths is a long tongue for catching **prey**.

▲ *Red-eyed tree frogs are **nocturnal**. They sleep during the day.*

Climbing trees

Like most other tree frogs, the red-eyed tree frog has **suction pads** on its fingers and toes. It uses them to grip as it climbs trees.

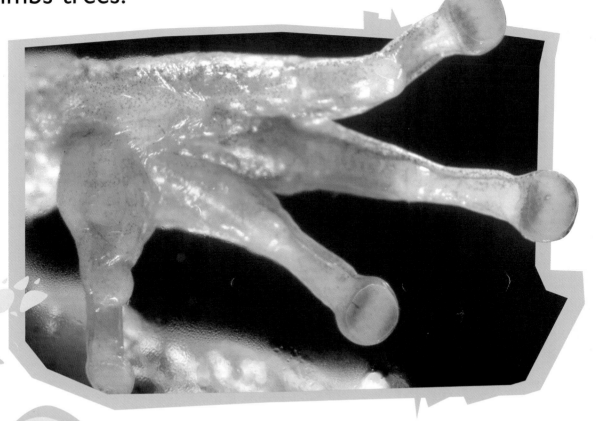

⏶ *The suction pads stick fast to wet leaves and branches.*

▲ *Tree frogs spend most of their time climbing.*

The frog's long, strong back legs help it climb and leap. It hops through the trees to find food. It hops down to lay its eggs.

Breathing

All frogs can breathe both in and out of the water. When they are out of the water they breathe with **nostrils** and **lungs**, just like us.

▲ *This tree frog has taken a deep breath, ready to **croak**.*

When frogs are under water they use their skin to breathe. **Gases** pass in and out through their skin, instead of through their nostrils.

▼ Red-eyed tree frogs can hide under water from **predators**.

Rainforest food

Red-eyed tree frogs hunt at night. They eat insects, such as beetles, moths, and flies. They also eat spiders. They catch their food with their long, sticky tongue.

▲ *A red-eyed tree frog sits quietly, waiting to take an insect by surprise.*

The frog uses its eyes to target its prey.

When an insect lands near by, the frog's tongue shoots out. The tongue grabs the **prey** and pulls it into the frog's mouth. The insect is swallowed whole.

Croaking in the forest

In autumn, the sound of **croaking** fills the **rainforest**. The **male** red-eyed tree frogs are ready to **mate**. They are croaking to attract **females**.

▼ Air fills up a sac in the frog's throat to make the croak sound louder.

When the male finds a female, he climbs on her back. She carries him down the tree. They go to find a place where she will lay her eggs.

The male is smaller than the female.

Laying eggs

Red-eyed tree frogs must lay their eggs near water. The **female** carries the **male** on her back until she finds a good place to lay her eggs.

⏶ *Females lay about 50 eggs. A group of eggs is called a clutch.*

After the eggs are laid, the male leaves the female. The female has to go down to the pond several times to get water to keep the eggs wet.

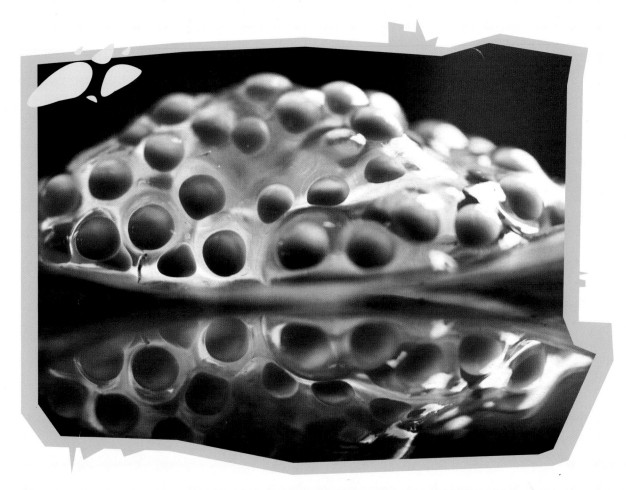

⏶ *The eggs must be kept wet. If they dry up, they will not hatch.*

Tadpoles

The eggs hatch after a few days. **Tadpoles** wriggle from the eggs, then drop into the pond below. Tadpoles can only breathe in water. They breathe through **gills**.

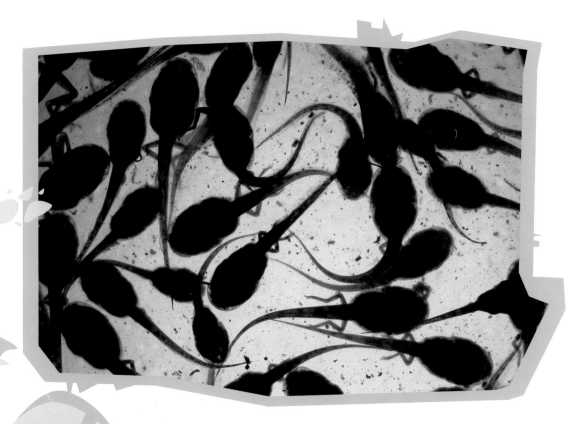

▲ *Tadpoles do not look like frogs. They are a different shape and colour.*

The tadpoles swim through the water. Slowly, they grow legs, and their tail gets smaller. This change from tadpole to frog is called **metamorphosis**.

▼ *Once the tadpoles become frogs, they can breathe out of the water.*

Hiding away

Many animals in the **rainforest** eat frogs. They are in danger from snakes, bats, and birds. Red-eyed tree frogs use their cat-like eyes to look out for **predators**.

▲ Many tree frogs sleep at night, but red-eyed tree frogs are awake.

During the day, the red-eyed tree frog might hide in a leaf. It pulls its legs close to its body and goes to sleep. **Camouflage** helps it to hide.

▼ *The frog's green body is hard to spot against a green leaf or plant.*

Bright colours

When a red-eyed tree frog is woken by a **predator**, it quickly opens its eyes. The sudden flash of its bright red eyes may frighten the predator away.

▼ *Would you be surprised if you saw these eyes?*

If the red-eyed tree frog sees a predator near by, it jumps away. The bright colours on its legs and sides surprise and confuse the predator.

▶▶ *This frog has time to jump away and hide while the predator is confused.*

Trees in danger

Large parts of the **rainforests** where tree frogs live are being cut down. Already, half the rainforests in the world are gone.

▲ *These logs came from trees that were cut down. They are used to build houses.*

Soon the tree frogs will have even fewer places to live. If they do not have anywhere to live they will die out.

▼ *Many people are working to protect rainforests.*

Tracker's guide

When you want to watch animals in the wild, you need to find them first. You can look for clues they leave behind.

◀◀ *If you listen carefully you might hear tree frogs **croaking**.*

◀◀ *You might be able to spot some tiny eggs on a leaf.*

▶▶ *If you look closely you might be able to see a tree frog on a leaf or flower.*

29

Glossary

amphibian animals such as frogs and salamanders. They can live under water and on land.

camouflage colours and patterns that hide an animal where it lives

croak loud sound that a frog makes

female animal that can become a mother when it is grown up. Girls and women are female people.

gas air is made up of gases that you cannot see

gills parts on either side of the body of a fish or tadpole that are used for breathing

habitat area where an animal usually lives

lungs parts inside the body that you use to breathe air in and out

male animal that can become a father when it is grown up. Boys and men are male people.

mate when male and female animals produce young

metamorphosis when an animal changes shape as it grows, such as a tadpole to a frog

nocturnal awake and active at night, asleep during the day

nostrils holes that you breathe through. Your nose has two nostrils.

predator animal that catches and eats other animals for food

prey animal that gets caught and eaten by other animals

rainforest place where many trees and plants grow close together and where lots of rain falls

suction pads cup-shaped feet and finger ends that stick to leaves and branches

tadpole young frog in the first stage of its life

Find out more

Books

Continents: South America, M. Fox (Heinemann Library, 2002)

Journey of the Red-Eyed Tree Frog, Martin and Tanis Jordan
      (Simon & Schuster, 1992)

Life Cycles: Frog, Claire Hibbert (Raintree, 2004)

Red-Eyed Tree Frog, Joy Cowley (Scholastic Press, 1999)

We're from Brazil, Vic Parker (Heinemann Library, 2005)

Why am I an amphibian? Greg Pyers (Raintree, 2005)

Why do animals have skin and scales? Elizabeth Miles
      (Heinemann Library, 2002)

Websites

Find out lots more exciting facts about red-eyed tree frogs at:
http://allaboutfrogs.org/info/species/redeye.html

Look at this website for useful information about these amazing creatures:
http://nationalgeographic.com/kids/creature_feature/0203/frogs.html

Disclaimer

All the internet addresses (URLs) given in this book were valid at the time of going to press.
However, due to the dynamic nature of the internet, some addresses may have changed, or sites
may have ceased to exist since publication. While the author and publishers regret any
inconvenience this may cause readers, no responsibility for such changes can be accepted by
either the author(s) or the publishers.

Index

Titles in the *Wild World* series include:

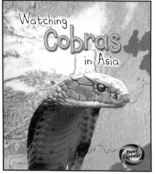

Hardback   0 431 19066 6

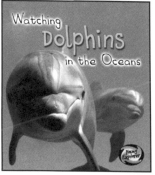

Hardback   0 431 19071 2

Hardback   0 431 19084 4

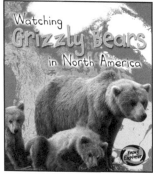

Hardback   0 431 19069 0

Hardback   0 431 19067 4

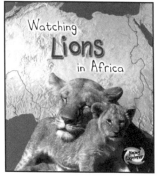

Hardback   0 431 19064 X

Hardback   0 431 19085 2

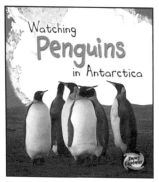

Hardback   0 431 19065 8

Hardback   0 431 19068 2

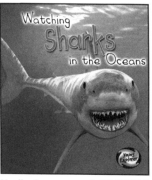

Hardback   0 431 19086 0

Hardback   0 431 19070 4

Find out about other Heinemann Library titles on our website www.heinemann.co.uk/library